Liberated Publishing Inc

Presents…

I0148985

Inspired from the Secret Place

www.liberatedpublishing.com

Liberated Publishing Inc.
1860 Wilma Rudolph Blvd
Clarksville, TN 37040

ISBN **978-0-982552391**

First Printing: June 2013

Printed in the United States of America

This book is dedicated to
All the ones I love. I could not have done this without
your support, faith, and constant encouragement.

~In Loving Memory of My Grandparents, Ms. Samella
Montgomery and Mr. & Mrs. David Sanders~

Acknowledgements

I must first acknowledge my Heavenly Father from whom all blessings flow. Thank you Lord because without you this wouldn't be possible but you specialize in the impossible and it is so. To my best half Carl A. Medley, every time I reach for your hand it is always there. Thank you so much for enduring this journey with me and being my rock. To the best part of me my children Centavius, Tandrea, Kihaina, and Raquan. Thank you for your thoughts, encouragement, and lending me your ears over and over (I know you all would say add a few more over's) again. To my parents Arthur L. Sanders and especially to my mother Prophetess Patricia A. Sanders for your constant empowerment, prayers, inspiration, and support. Also for teaching me to believe in God, myself, and in my dreams. Thank you mother dearest. Thank you to my superheroes Antonio, Jethro, and Trey. Your special powers are being great and awesome brothers. Always by my side and a text away (smile). Thank you to my Aunt Minister Darlene Smith and especially to my Aunt Prophetess Daphne Radcliffe for building me up, being my biggest encourager, your assistance, and for just simply always being there for me. To my cousins, Michele Garrett my twin (insider) and Karen Howard, thank you. To my best friend for life Alfreda Horn-Knight, thank you for being my prayer partner, believing in and with me, listening to my poems, and most of all always being a true friend. To my best and dear friend Stephanie Wilson for seeing the best in me, listening, and for your enthusiasm in my poems that helped motivate me to continue to write, thanks. Last but certainly not least, a big thank you to my editor Deja Floyd. I love each and every one of you. Again, thank you!

6

Preface

To God I give all the honor, the praise, and the glory for what He has done. For I've never thought of myself as a poet, but God. Inspired from the Secret Place is a collection of poems that were inspired by God. This book is based on the wisdom of God's word from being thankful when on the mountain top to knowing how to stand when in the valley. These poems were written to inspire, give hope, and spiritual encouragement as you face the trials of life whether it be sickness, death of a loved one, loneliness, hurt or discouragement. No matter what issues you are faced with don't quit but continue to move forward. For the trying of your faith worketh patience and patience produces power. Knowing that all things work together for good to them that love God, to them who are the called according to his purpose.

Thankfulness

Give Thanks

Every now and then you have to tell God Thank you

Thank God for keeping you in your right mind
You thought you would lose it cause peace you couldn't find
When you felt like you couldn't take life anymore
God kept you and your joy He did restore
The times He made a way out of no way
Even the times when you went astray
Thank Him for the times He protected you
From danger you couldn't see from your view
Providing food to make a meal
Restoring your health the devil wanted to steal
Healing you from past hurt and pain
Giving you a promotion man couldn't explain
Thank Him for blessing you with your kids and spouse
Blessing you with a car and your beautiful house
In everything give thanksgiving
Thank Him for the life you're living

If I Had Ten Thousand Tongues I Couldn't Thank You Enough

Let's take a moment to look back over our life

-Pause-

Now that we've looked back and the spirit of thanksgiving fills
our heart
I can't help offering up a sacrifice of praise unto God
Thank you
Thank you
Thank you Lord

Still meditating on His goodness
I clap my hands
I do a few hand waves
Hallelujah Lord I give you the highest praise
Thank you
Thank you
Thank you
Stirring up the gift
The atmosphere just did a shift

Thank you coming out much faster
Thank you thank you thank you thank you thank you thank you
Tears running down my face
I'm just so thankful for your mercy and grace
Thank you thank you thank you thank you thank you thank you
Feels like fire shut up in my bones
So intense it makes me groan
I let out one loud sharp piercing cry
I praise you God you are the most high
I take off running and begin to dance
Thanking and praising God like it's my last chance

If I Never

If I never had bad days
I wouldn't be thankful for the good ones
If I never went through
I wouldn't know coming out only makes you stronger
If I never been tested
I wouldn't have a testimony
If I never was knocked down
I wouldn't know how to stand
If I never was lost
I couldn't have been found
If I never hungered or thirst
I wouldn't be filled
If I've never been tired
I wouldn't know how to rest in Him
If I never been chastised
I wouldn't have known His love
If I never had a dry season
Latter rain wouldn't have fallen
If I never had a door closed
I wouldn't recognize the one God opened
If I never been sick
I wouldn't have met Christ the healer
If I never been broke
I wouldn't know Jehovah Jireh as my provider
If I never was in the valley low
I wouldn't have had a mountain top experience
If I never was bound
I couldn't have been made free
If I never prayed
I wouldn't know God answers prayers
If I never forgave
I wouldn't be forgiven
If I never stepped out

Faith wouldn't have showed up
If I never wept
Joy couldn't have came in the morning
If I never was faced with the impossible
I wouldn't have met the miracle worker
If I never was on the battlefield
I wouldn't know to put on the whole armor of God
If I never read the bible
I wouldn't know who I am
If I never had a storm
I wouldn't know I could speak to one
If Jesus had never died
My name couldn't be found in the book of life
If I never was fearfully and wonderfully made
You wouldn't be reading this

No More Crumbs

There once was a land called not enough
Where the folks lived broke as a joke
The sun doesn't shine and the rain never falls
No way out, they were surrounded by brick walls

One day a man went wandering in the wilderness
He saw an old shabby rickety well
Curious, he leaned over and inside he fell

Now crippled, he awakens to see a wooden door
He hopped on one foot and through it he explored
Realizing it's an underground hideaway
Faster and more quickly he limps all the way
His eyes he squint from the sun rays
Amazed because he never saw a sunny day

He reached the end and what did he see
A land flowing with milk and honey

No more crumbs the broke man thought, it's time to take a seat
Time for me to enjoy richly, a rich man's feast

Praise and Worship

Present your body a living and holy sacrifice
That's your reasonable service of worship in life
No person or thing only God as the center
Thanksgiving at the gates is how you enter
Come into his courts with true praise
Glorifying and exalting God throughout your days
You must worship in spirit and in truth
Obedience to God and His word is the root
God inhabits the praise of His people
From the rising of the sun until the going down of the same
If you hold your peace the rocks will cry out in your name
Praise Him for His wonderful works and goodness
Pour out adoration and thankfulness
Draw closer to God through praise, worship, and humbleness
It's not because you expect Him to do something
But because of who He is you give Him the Praise

-Excuse me for a moment while I praise and worship Him-

You are rich in grace and mercy
My prince of peace
My strong tower
Forgiver of my sins
As the deer pants for water my soul pants for you
I just had to give honor to where honor was due
I pray you took a moment to honor Him too

Remember-
Reverence the Lord, Lift up holy hands
Bow before Him, kneel, or stand
Run, jump, dance, or lay prostrate
Satan powers are broken when you celebrate
Worship the Lord in the beauty of holiness
He is magnificent and glorious

16

Bless the Lord at all times
His praise shall continually be in your mouth

Question: What moment in your life that every time you think about it you just can't help but to say thank you God?

_____

_____

_____

_____

_____

_____

_____

_____

Bible Verse: Give praise to the LORD, proclaim his name; make known among the nations what he has done. Sing to him, sing praise to him; tell of all his wonderful acts. *Psalm 105:1-2*

Faith

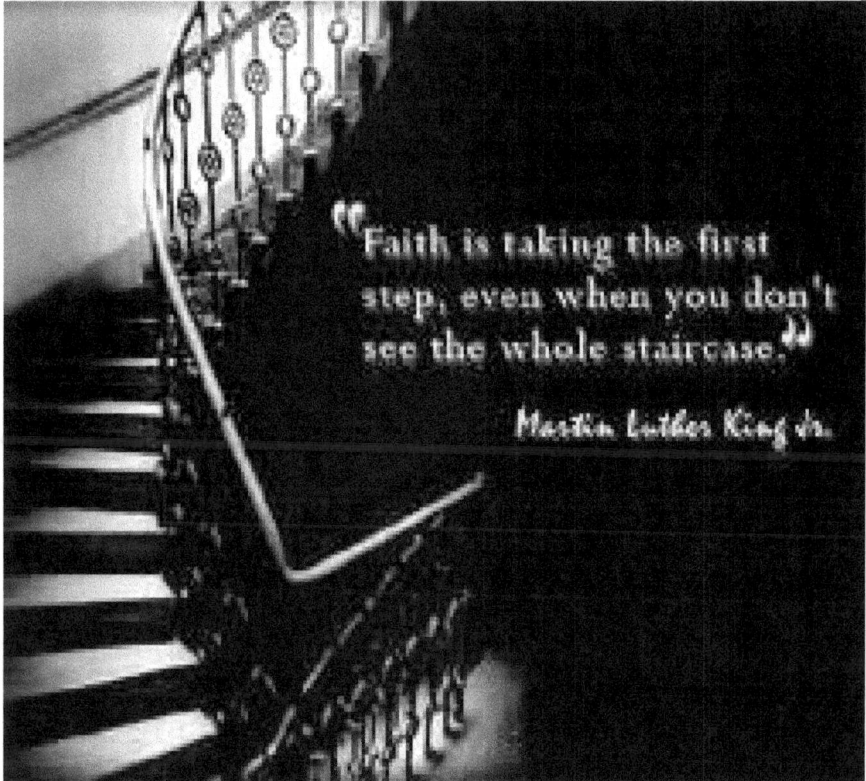

"Faith is taking the first step, even when you don't see the whole staircase."

Martin Luther King Jr.

Antidote

You go to see your physician
He comes in and asks what are your symptoms
You say, head hurts, heart palpitations, ringing in your ears
Your eyes are straining, puffy, and this redness just appeared
Arthritis in your hands, feet swollen, and you have back pain
I couldn't bear it anymore so to you I came
He thoroughly checks you out
Says your head hurts from doubt
Your ears have not been hearing the word
Your heart you did not guard from what you saw and heard
Your eyes have not been fixed
Which has caused you to be betwixt
You haven't been fighting with your sword
So arthritis in the bones has been stored
Your feet haven't been shoded with the preparation of peace
Back pain from the weight of the world that you need to release
I'm going to prescribe an antidote:
Trust In the Lord and On Him You Wait
Immediately take a double dose of faith
Every day all day take the word to get it in your system
Continue daily to pray without ceasing
When you start to feel better do not stop
Everyday this pill you must pop
To prevent this reoccurring deadly bug
Fasting is the probiotic drug
Living water will overflow your cup
Follow the directions and you won't need a follow-up

Faith

Don't push
Don't run
Walk
Walk by faith and not by sight
Step by step in the direction He will light
For we are saved by faith
We live by faith
We stand firm in our belief in faith
We receive the promises of God by faith
We are justified in Christ by faith
We access God's grace by faith
We are waiting for Christ to return by faith
Faith is very important and vital to a Christian's life indeed
Faith the grain of a mustard seed is all that you need
Faith is being sure of what we hope for and certain of what we do
not see
Faith is where the works of God are made real to those that
believe

Faithful Runner

On your mark, get set, go
Run at your on tempo
Don't look back, to the left, or the right
Keep your eyes focused on Christ

Tests are not made to destroy you
The fiery furnace you must go through
Don't stop running in the middle of the race
Don't throw in the towel, keep the pace
Run across the finish line to hear well done
When you were weak, I was made strong
I allowed all the right and wrong
Not one day did you ever run alone
Enter in O'faithful one
A room in my mansion is now your home

Receive It

I receive all that God has for me
To walk in my spiritual authority
To command a thing and it will be so
To walk in greatness and be bold

I receive all that God has for me
When sickness attacks my body
I receive His healing power
The power that heals this very hour

I receive all that God has for me
When the adversary comes in like a flood
I receive he will deliver me
My God will raise a standard against the enemy

I receive all that God has for me
No more lack just prosperity
No bondage through Christ I'm set free
Peace, Joy, and love
I have a right of
Wholeness and nothing broken
I receive all that I've spoken
Whatever God has for me is for me
His promises are yea and amen so it shall be
I receive all that God has for me
Make it personal and say amen if you agree

Stand During the Test

In our test God is building patience and perseverance
He is teaching us to rely, lean, and trust in Him
To stand during the test when our way looks dim
While we're being built to stand during the test
An attitude of praise must be what we express
It may seem as if he's taking way too long
Just know He gives His hardest test to the strong
God's timing is not like ours
He created the day, night, and the hours
He doesn't come early and He's never late
He's just teaching us to stand during our wait
God wants to show Himself big, so never doubt
He will perform a miracle when He shows up to show out

The Fight

You're in the ring
The bell goes ding
Test and trials on every side
Done all you can, you prayed and cried
A hit below the belt knocked you down
The enemy thinks he's getting the crown
One
The devil's having fun
Two
Steady kicking you
Three
Jesus help me
Four
You're still at war
Five
Bloody but alive
Six
Your eyes are fixed
Seven
Departs heaven
Eight
You kept the faith
Nine
Right on time
Ten
God caused you to win

Vision

Habakkuk 2:3 write the vision down
It is for a future time
It describes the end
Although it may seem slow in coming don't bend
Wait patiently, it will take place
Stay in the I claim it race
It won't be delayed it shall come to pass
If God spoke it, speak it, only His word will last
God is a God who doesn't lie
It will be fulfilled don't let your vision die

Question: How are you able to stand when you want to give up?

_____

_____

_____

_____

_____

_____

_____

_____

Because you know that the testing of your faith produces perseverance. *James 1:3*

Forgiveness

"To forgive is to set a prisoner free and discover that the prisoner was you."

— Lewis Smedes

Forgiven

In the death of Christ our sinful self-received the wages of sin
The resurrection of Christ gave us a new life to begin
Amazing what God did through our savior Jesus Christ
Sin is forgiven, His only son paid the ultimate sacrifice
Confess and believe boldly in forgiveness of your sin
For the blood of Jesus never fails it always wins
The enemy tries to tell us, God will not forgive
No condemnation, be free, trust His grace, get up and live
Get up and live in the SONshine of God's grace
For a just man falls seven times but gets up to finish the race
Confident in the blood that Jesus Christ shed
Remembering no more, forgiven, your sin is now dead

Unforgiveness

"It's so unfair for them to receive forgiveness to be set free
You don't know what they did and afflicted upon me"

Unforgiveness in your heart is like pouring rain
You're aching from all the unforgiven hurt and pain
Unforgiveness is running throughout each vein
Defiling your mind, leaving a don't forgive them stain
Harboring on what they've done, you drink again from the poison
cup
Now toxic in your body is all built up
You're sick and oppressed
Stressed and depressed
Distressed and suppressed
Unforgiveness has you possessed
Taken away to solitary prison
Unforgiveness accomplished its mission
Jailed with bitter, meanness, anguish, and hate
Chained to an atomic ticking bomb weight
All because you were captured by the unforgiven bait
Unforgiveness corroding all of your bones
Its grave crying for you with its moans and groans

Unforgiveness Prayer

Heavenly Father, I come to you in Jesus name
I no longer want to remain the same
You cried out on the cross forgive them for they know not what
they do
Instill within me the kind of love that releases people's debts too
The wrong that was afflicted upon me still hurts deep within
Remove the roots so that by the power of your spirit healing can
begin
I release to you debts I have held over the heads who have
wronged me
Forgive me for walking in unforgiveness as I forgive them please
Set me free from my bondage of unforgiveness and bitterness
I want no part that hinders my walk on the path of righteousness
Whenever those weeds of unforgiveness try to surface
Remind me that you love them as much as you love me
Remind me of the times that I wronged and sinned against thee
Remind me that you took my place
So that I can now obtain mercy and grace
I thank you Lord that I am now free from the unforgiveness
prison
This day I set my debtor free, you are now forgiven
Jesus name, Amen

Question: Is there anyone you need to release from the bond of unforgiveness? Is there anyone you need to ask to forgive you?

_____

_____

_____

_____

_____

_____

_____

Get rid of all bitterness, rage and anger, brawling and slander, along with every form of malice. [32] Be kind and compassionate to one another, forgiving each other, just as in Christ God forgave you.
Ephesians 4:31-32

Trust God

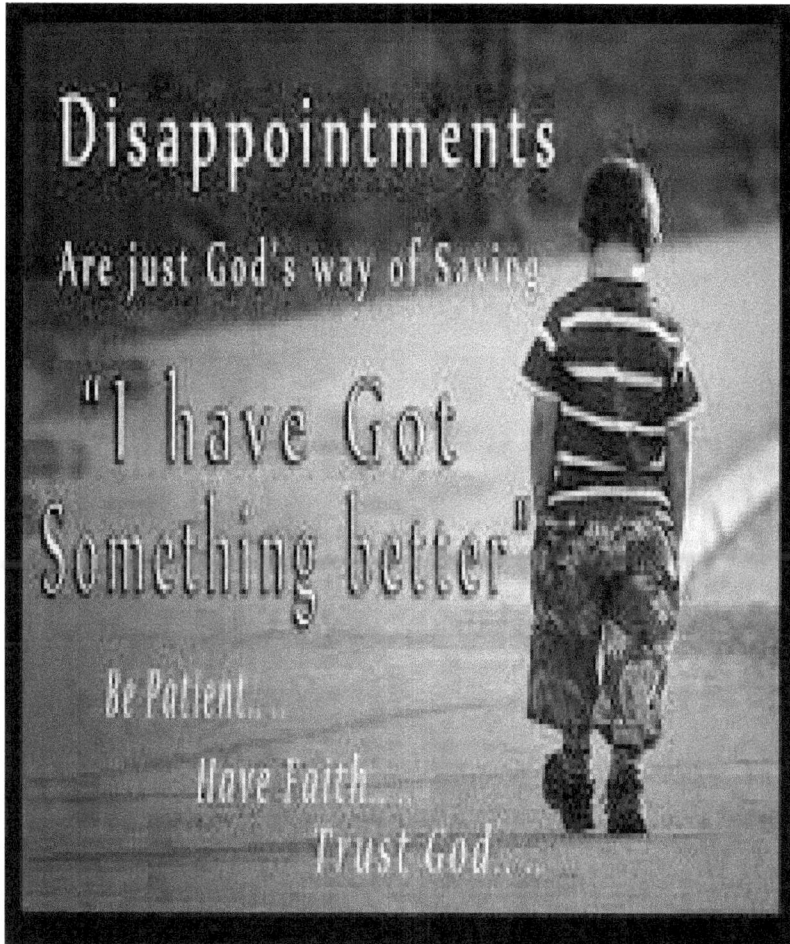

All Things Work Together For Our Good

Those who love God and who are called according to His plan
It all works together for our good, anything that happens to man
Failure of a relationship, victim of rape, or years of abuse by a
loved one's hand
Prison, drugs, alcohol, death of a daughter or son, answers you
demand
How in the world can He work that out for my good, how can that
be
We may not know why or understand, like it at the moment, or
even agree
What we do know is God's word is true and His word we must
decree
We must trust God because He is always faithful to do what He
says He will do
All things work together for our good even when we can't see our
way through
Our Father knows what is best for us, His ways is not our own
He sees the master plan although to us it's unknown
All things work together for our good according to His plan
Be confident that He is faithful to finish the work in which He
began

God of Promise

People change
Weather change
God remains the same

God is not a man that He should lie
If He spoke it you can rely

God's word is true
His promises are too

God's word stands firm forever
Settled in heaven to be changed never

Heaven and earth will pass
God's word is the only thing that will last

God is a God whose word can't fail
What He says will prevail

All of His works are just
The word of the Lord you can entrust

Whatever promise you are standing upon
Mix your faith with it no matter how long
Satan will come to you with a lie
God does it for others but you He will deny
He that is faithful is able to perform it, stagger not at the promises
of God through unbelief
Remember to stand on the word of God until your blessing is
released

God Said It I Believe It

God said it
I believe it
That settles it
I don't have to write a poem that's long
I go before almighty God whose sitting on the throne
I Confess and believe and it's done in Jesus name
God said it I believe it and you must do the same

He Sees All

The woman that woke up and gave thanks
The man who blames life for his mistake
The mother praying on her knees
The daughter that's prostituting to meet her needs
The father who's working hard to provide
The son that's on the corner outside
The victim rocking in the padded room
The pregnant lady worried about the baby in her womb
The grandmother that's humming gospel hymns
The soldier that lost two of his limbs
The judge that makes life changing decisions
The inmate that hung himself in prison
The president striving to lead the nation
Sexual acts that's an abomination
The pastor seeking a word for his flock
The masked robber that picked the lock
The house that burned all the way down
The hung low head that wears a frown
The one that's in the hospital bed
The car wreck that left one dead
The one that's going left and not right
Those tears that kept you up all night
No matter what it is He sees all
Even the tempter who caused man to fall
Nothing clears without being reviewed
Charges His angels to watch over me and you
Gives us the strength to make it through

Never Seen Him Fail

I have never seen Him show up late
He has always delivered and showed Himself great

I have never seen Him fail
I've stood on His word and watch his word prevail
I've never seen the righteous forsaken or seed begging bread
Is there anything too hard for me is what the Lord said

He has made my crooked ways straight
Specialize in the impossible
I've seen Him move mountains
I've seen His healing power
I've seen Him turn the heart of man
To bring to pass His purpose and plan
I've seen Him open a closed door
Put relationships back together and restore
I've seen Him turn a no into yes
People say I'm lucky but I call it blessed

I've never seen Him fail

Put It in Jesus Hands

Difficulties
Anxiety
Anger
Rage
From trauma that happened to you at a young age
Eating disorder
Depression
Bad temper
Fears
That has had you paralyzed all these years
Job stress
Pride
Drug addiction
Smoking
Pornography
Strife
From seeing bitter conflicts, violence, and arguing your parents did all your life
Whatever your issues are that have caused you to fall away and not stand
You must mentally take a moment to put those issues in your hand
Now mentally put them in the out stretched hands of our Father and pray
Heavenly Father, I give you this matter solidly in your hands this day
That no evil can penetrate it one bit
By putting your shield of protection around it
Thank you Jesus for taking care of this matter today
In Jesus great and mighty name I pray

Now that it is placed in God's hands leave it there
When you are tempted remind yourself it's no longer yours to bear
You gave it to our Heavenly Father in prayer

Question: How have your storms and valleys helped make you into the person you are today?

_____

_____

_____

_____

_____

_____

_____

_____

Call those things which be not as though they were. *Romans 4:17*

In God's Image

You were created in God's image. God makes no mistakes.

To put yourself down for the way you are is to insult God's handiwork.

You are beautiful.

God's Masterpiece...Who Me

It can't be right I don't feel like a masterpiece
It can't be right I don't look like a masterpiece
How can it be I do more wrong then right
A misfortune I must be in Gods marvelous sight
A still voice says, Ephesians two ten
You are my masterpiece regardless of your sin
Gods masterpiece...who me
Look in the mirror and see what I see
A prized possession what I created you to be
You're unique, an original, you're one of a kind
Created in my image for a purpose you were designed
Your life may look simple, plain, and ordinary
You must understand who you are and whose you are, everything
else is contrary
I created the moon, the stars, heaven, and the earth
You are my finishing touch, my greatest work of art, predestined
since birth
I've placed in you gifts, talents, and rich treasure
You're the apple of my eye of whom I take great pleasure
I've called you to leave an artistic mark, so dare to be bold
Behold my masterpiece, priceless, worth more than gold

Look At You Now

Look at where God has brought you from
Look at what He has delivered you out of
He reached down just to show His everlasting love
He lifted you out of the slimy pit, mud, and mire clay
You're thinking to yourself right now "Oh what a day"
He washed you clean and made you free
Cast your sins in the forgetfulness sea
He sat your feet up on a rock and gave you a firm place to stand
You've been running the race ever since, holding on to His hand

Can't nobody tell it like you can tell your own story
You're not what you use to be but look at you now, being used
for God's glory

Through Holy Eyes

Natural eyes cannot see
All that the spirit reveals to me
Through Holy eyes I can see
The real you and what you were meant to be
Natural eyes all that can be seen
Is a filthy fleshy human being
Through holy eyes it's been disguised
I see the robe of righteousness
Placed on you by the most high
Natural eyes see all you've done
Not the right just the wrong
Constantly keeping it before your face
Through holy eyes I see God's grace
The sin is not remembered it's been erased
I hear God saying run on finish your race
Natural eyes can only see
The just man fall when he got weak
Through holy eyes you can see
God's waiting for him at the mercy seat
Judge, talk, hold me at fault
You haven't been where I've walked
Carnal minded man can't understand
The sacrifice of the lamb
I've been bought at a cost
Jesus came to save all who's lost
We've all fallen and came short of His glory
There shouldn't be one of us without a story
Natural eyes see the outer appearance
Through holy eyes it's about the heart within us
Love covers a multitude of sin
So how much love have you showed toward men
It was love that lifted and kept me
From sinking deep in a sinful sea

The natural eyes cannot see
The blood of Jesus that covers me
Through holy eyes I've been set free
I've been given the victory

Tick Tock

Behold I stand at the door and knock
You hear God speaking but His voice you block
Tick tock tick tock tick tock
Time is running out on your spiritual clock
From your calling you continue to run
The world is offering nothing but fun
Drinking, sex, and a party life style
You feel God tugging at your heart all the while
Tick tock tick tock tick tock
Time is running out on your spiritual clock
God uses your christian friend to minister the word
You think the whole concept of being a christian is absurd
She says, choose you this day whom you will serve
Her preaching is already getting on your last nerve
She continues to say God loves you and gave His only begotten
son
He's able to finish the work in you that He has begun
The death road you're on to you seems right
Our God is calling you out of darkness into His light
God rather you be cold or hot
For at a high price you were bought
You are of your father the devil
You think to yourself, I never thought about it on that level
You must work while it is day
You hear God's knock, I am the way
No man can serve two masters
Go and show yourself to a pastor

You've repented, been baptized, and now made free
Born again, you've been given the kingdom key

Excited you're a CHRISTIAN now, you go and tell your friend
She warns you there will still be times that you run into a dead
end
You will have tests, trials, and shed tears on some days
But don't let the devil steal your praise
Storms will come and the wind will blow
The word of God you must know
Put on the whole armor of God to be able to stand
Eternal life, never to perish, forever in His hand

Transform Me

I don't want to be the way I am
There are areas in me I need to change
I've been trying all on my own
Putting off the old man wanting him to be gone
I lift my hands to surrender my all
Lord please hear my humble call

Transform me transform me
Make me more like you
Through and through and through
Transform me transform me
In your image is how I want to be

You are the potter I am the clay
Mold me into what you would have me to be
Create in me a new heart
Renew the right spirit within me
Remove the heart of stone and give me a heart of flesh
Lord restore me and refresh

Transform me transform me
Make me more like you
Through and through and through
Transform me transform me
In your image is how I want to be

I offer myself as a living sacrifice
Change the way I think
Make my mind anew
I want to be an imitation and look just like you
Transform me transform me
By your word and the power of the Holy Spirit, transform me

The Two Builders

There are two kinds of builders
The foolish and the wise
One digs deep and the other compromise

The wise man digs through layers of gravel, dirt, and sand
His house is securely anchored to the rock to be able to withstand
He anticipated there would be stormy days that only the rock
could sustain
He knew the rock wouldn't wash away in the flood or crumble in
the rain

The foolish man will take a look at a sight
Begins to build even if it's not right
He doesn't anchor the house on anything other than vulnerable
sand
Which will easily wash away, his building was unplanned

The wise man takes the blocks of Jesus word
Responds in obedience to what he heard
It becomes a part of his everyday life
Even through the hard and trying times he is committed to doing
what's right
The foolish man hears and understands
Goes to church and refuses to do what the Lord commands

Both builders want a house that's secure
But only one builds on a foundation that'll endure

Foolish or wise which are you
The time will come will yours stand or fall through

You Are

You are created in God's image
Justified and redeemed
Set free from sin and death
Fearfully and wonderfully made
Your sins He paid
You are a new creature in Christ
The seed of Abraham
Chosen
An heir
Blameless
Of a royal priesthood
Because in your place He stood
You are God's workmanship
Sealed with the promise
Seated in heavenly places
Called out of darkness and into the light
Keys to the kingdom is your birthright
You are more than a conqueror
Above and not beneath
The lender and not the borrower
Blessed and not cursed
The head and not the tail
The gates of hell shall not prevail
You are a child of the bright and morning star
You are who God says you are

Question: Did you ever think you would be where you are in Christ today? Why or why not?

_____

_____

_____

_____

_____

_____

_____

_____

You, dear children, are from God and have overcome them, because the one who is in you is greater than the one who is in the world. *1John 4:4*

Praying Power

PLUG INTO THE POWER OF PRAYER

Pray the Word

When the doctor has given you six months to live
Isaiah 53:5 by your stripes I am healed
Wrongfully done and you want to attack
Romans 12:19 vengeance is mine I will repay back
Working hard and still not enough to get by
Philippians 4:19 all my needs my God will supply
You just don't know what they did to me
Matthew 6:14 forgive so that your Heavenly Father can forgive
thee
Nothing around you is going right
2 Corinthians 5:7 walk by faith and not by sight
Protection over you and your family all of your days
Psalm 91:11 He will give His angels charge to watch over you in
all your ways
Worrying, unpleasant thoughts, and you don't know what else to
do
Isaiah 26:3 you will keep in perfect peace whose mind is stayed
on you
The enemy trying to remind you of what you use to be
Galatians 5:1 Christ has set us free
Weighed down and your view is dim
1 Peter 5:7 cast all your burdens upon Him
You need direction in your life every day
Psalm 119:105 your word is a lamp to light my way

Find and pray the word for what you need
For in the word you will find what you need to succeed

Proclamation power

You may not be able to see your way right now because of life
issues
Abandonment, hurt, or abuse that caused you to be broken
Negative hurtful words over your life that was spoken
Accused or wrongly done
Death of a loved one
Not enough money to pay your bills
You're looking but you see no hills
A bad report from the doctor that you've suddenly heard
You're trying to see Jesus in the midst but your vision is blurred
The devil been messing with you all week long
That seems to be your new theme song
But I declare you must sing what God says
You must speak His word
Despite what you've been through or the evil report you've heard
We have the power to call those things that be not as though they
are
You must proclaim healing of past hurts that every open wound is
now a scar
There is power in proclamation of the word
Let the word be your war cry
God watches over His word and He cannot lie

Proclamation means to announce, cry, call out, or declare
Proclaim that all your burdens God will bear
Proclaim all your needs, God will supply
Proclaim healing that you shall live and not die
Proclaim a table before your enemies that God will prepare
You must break and lose the bands of the wicked one through
warfare
Proclaim to the devil that out of his hands you've been redeemed
Proclaim to the devil that he has no power and the blood of Jesus is
over me
Proclaim beauty instead of ashes
Oil of gladness instead of mourning

Proclaim a garment of praise instead of a spirit of despair
Remind God of His promises through intercessory prayer
There is power in proclamation of the word
Know that you are strong in the Lord and in the power of His might
That no weapon formed shall prosper and your battles God will fight
SHOUT with a voice of triumph until your Jericho wall falls down
Know that you are triumphant and no longer bound
Throughout all the earth you must become a loud megaphone
Proclamation of the word must be made known

The Prayer

I come before you in the name above every name
Your worthy and awesome, your praises I proclaim
I thank you for manifesting what is already done
Not only in my life but in everyone's
I thank you for providing all of today's needs
My store house is full I declare and decree
One by one I do confess
Forgiving those who have transgress
Wash and renew the right spirit within me
As I hide your word in my heart that I sin not against thee
You have enlarged my steps so my feet won't slip
Destroying the bands of temptations evil grip
No weapon formed against me will prevail
Those that rise against me shall fail
You said you will never leave nor forsake me
Under the blood is where I always want to be
I am trusting you, keeping the faith, and staying in your will
I thank you for fighting my battles as I stand still
I thank you for the victory and being my strong tower
I give you all the glory and honor for your omnipotent power

Where Two Agree

Anything that concerns you, make your petition known
Find a believer with faith to go with you before the throne
The bible says it shall be done if two of you shall agree
Put God in remembrance of His word and so shall it be

Question: How has praying turned a situation around for you?

_____

_____

_____

_____

_____

_____

_____

_____

And I will do whatever you ask in my name, so that the Father may be glorified in the Son. [14] You may ask me for anything in my name, and I will do it. John 14:13-14

Our Weakness His Strength

when i am
weak,
HE IS
STRONG

Afflictions

Afflictions cause us to depend on God
Motivates us to pray
Afflictions can be the wake-up call to seek God every day

Afflictions give us the desire to fulfill God's purpose for our life
It equips us, makes us strong, and wise
Afflictions take us to the fellowship place where God hears our cries

Afflictions can make life look hopeless
Has no respect of person, anybody it will attack
Afflictions prove the word works and is not a set back

Don't weep in the face of afflictions
Consider it pure joy whenever you go through a trial
All things will work together for your good in just a little while

Brokenness

Inside of us there can be areas of brokenness
From a broken relationship
From a broken dream
From a broken spirit
Even our self-esteem can be broken

A broken heart can hold us back from an authentic relationship of love
A broken spirit finds it virtually impossible to experience real joy from above
Broken self-esteem can stop us from exemplifying a positive personality that we're deprived of
How do we deal with brokenness in our lives
Do we mask it and pretend all is well to survive
In order to deal with brokenness it requires the truth
We must admit to what's broken we have to find the root
Was it a broken dream that was your dream and not in God's plan
Maybe a broken relationship that wasn't ordained because he wasn't a God sent man
As long as we rely on our own self and lust after the flesh
We will continue to live a broken life that won't be refreshed
Brokenness stops at the point where our spirit yields to Gods will
It's through our brokenness the need for God is revealed
Let your brokenness be perfected by Him
God's ultimate goal is spiritual victory and not a future that's dim
God is able to take your broken pieces and fit them together tightly
Never to be broken again once you surrender it all to the almighty

Dawn

In the midst of your dark gloomy night
Where problems are coming left and right
You're trying to feel and see your way through
Darkness so black it blocks your view
Gird up your loins and be still
Your darkness is just a temporary drill
God is on the way with your blessing, hold on
It's always darkest just before dawn
Arise and shine the light has come

Desolate Place

God knows all about your desolate place and He will guide you through

You may not be able to trace His hand but His eyes are upon you

Take comfort that there is no desolation that keeps you out of His vision

Whatever desolate place you're in God will make provision

He knows all about your trouble and He will guide you until the day is done

There's no friend like the lowly Jesus I haven't found one

He has the power to reach deep inside of your suffering, hurt, and pain

In your desert dry desolate place God can cause it to rain

You also have power, more power and strength then you know

Stand bold, stand firm, stand defiant in your desolation and command your mountain to go

Don't wait for the Lord to bring you out start thanking Him for moving your mountain

Don't let your desolation drown out your praise but let it spring forth like a fountain

Don't wait for the Lord to deliver you out of your desolate place

Raise your hand, shout hallelujah, and thank God for His grace

Your praise will cause God to enter in and everything broken He will restore

Pick you up, breathe new life into your dry place, and open a closed door

There is no secret to what our almighty God can do

What He does for one, He will do the same for you

The Storm

Storms come in different ways
Sickness, finances, or through your boss
Kids, marriage, or a loved one loss
Too much to carry burdened down
A storm will leave chaos all around
Heartbroken, lonely, or feeling defeated
A storm can cause your strength to be depleted

It's cloudy
It's dark
The wind is blowing hard

It's lightening
It's thundering
The storm came without watch or warning

Raindrops begin to fall
You look for cover to find none at all

The winds are stronger
Lightening more severe
You ask the question God do you care

The thunder rumbling makes your foundation shake
Suddenly it's pouring down and the storm you can't take

You remember the words peace be still and God has the last say
No matter what you speak the storm yet doesn't go away

You call out to God, eyes filled with tears
He comforts you and says, I am here
I have been with you all along
I'm just making you mighty and strong
It's stormy now but it'll soon be light
Your rainbow will come, shining bright

Stay in faith don't let the storm cause you to waiver
I've already covered you in my favor
Weapons that are formed are not of me
The devil desires to sift you as wheat
You have everything to make it on the inside
You will come out as gold after you've been tried
I will give you a powerful testament story
The storms and trying times are all for my glory

God has spoken and changed your whole view
You now begin to praise your way through

The Valley

The valley is a place of personal brokenness and weakness
A place of lowliness and meekness
The valley is the place where our faith is put to the test
It speaks of life's darker experiences a place of no rest
You feel so far from God's presence that you feel empty and
alone
The valley is so hard you weep, moan, and groan
You are desperately reaching and crying out to Christ
He ministers, the anointing comes at a price
Weeping may endure for just a night
But joy comes in the morning light
Your mountain top experience was to prepare you for your valley
low
To stretch your faith for you to spiritually grow
My grace is greater than your weakness, press your way don't
stop
I am the same God in the valley that was on the mountain top

Never despise your valley experience
You meet Christ, you are refreshed, and receive answers to your
prayers
You also come to know God through your experience of being the
God of everywhere

Question: How have your storms and valleys helped make you into the person you are today?

_____

_____

_____

_____

_____

_____

_____

_____

And the God of all grace, who called you to his eternal glory in Christ, after you have suffered a little while, will himself restore you and make you strong, firm and steadfast. *1Peter 5:10*

Don't Quit

NEVER GIVE UP
Go over, go under, go around, or go through.
But never give up.

God Speaks During the Rain

It's raining
It's raining
It's raining means hurtful tears are constantly falling
The flashflood on the inside causes your eyes to get all watery
Every time you cry its blood in your tears
But God touches them and says my love is here
Purged one by one you see them fall clear
I know your pain and feel your emotional need
Your tears are just watering that love needing seed
For I am God and I see the day you will no longer cry
For I will speak to the flash flood and command it to dry
Remember I told you not to complain
Double for your trouble in exchange
Now praise me my dear child for what I am about to do
All I need is your willing vessel to show my power through

Mask

If it wasn't for Covergirl or Maybelline
The bruises from pain could be seen
You wake up to paint a happy face on
It's just a mask until you get back home
While you're out you have to pretend
Temporarily bitterness and you become friends
Your mask conceals the wounds so no one can see
Unveiled the severity is third degree
The hurt is deeply buried alive
The taunting thoughts causes it to survive

How do you mask your bruises from pain
Pretend to walk around sound and sane
Temporarily befriending your open wounds
Covering the unseen marks on you
Unveiled what would we see
Another masked victim with third degree

The good news is you don't have to remain the same
There is healing in Jehovah –Rapha name
Give God all your hurt and pain
Take the mask off and let wholeness reign

Not One More Day

The issues of life
The weight of the world
Heavy burdened down feeling like a wind whirl
Home is not a home but a divided house
Your lover is now your enemy and despised spouse
Your kids are unruly, disobedient, and out of control
You feel like your sinking in a deep black hole
Yet you continue to get up and fight
Still the same story all darkness and no light
Feeling like you can't go on one more day
Not one more day
Not one more day
The pain of trials make you feel like a total cast away
The ones who are suppose to care
Are the same ones who aren't there
Family members to your best friend
Your left or right no one to depend
Wondering why so much to bear
Month after month, year after year
Face in your pillow as tears begin to flow
The devil hits you with his best blow
Just end it all to escape the pain
No more heavy weight from the ball and chain
No way out all doors are closed
You hear a different voice saying, satan you're exposed
You feel a peace fill the atmosphere
God tells you have no fear
Cast all your burdens and cares on me
Resist the devil and he will flee
Satan's power is always in a lie
On me you must totally rely
My grace is sufficient, come to the mercy seat
My power is made perfect when you are weak
To the strong I give the hardest test
Come to Me and I'll give you rest

The Answers to the Question

Can you tell me about your father?
He sits high and looks low
He took my place, paying a debt He didn't owe
Came in the flesh, died, and rose the third day
He is the life, the truth, and the way
Love, peace, and joy
My enemies He will destroy
He knows the number of my hairs
My burdens He does bear
More than one chance
My strong tower
All knowing and all powerful
He is always on time
Alpha and Omega
The author and finisher
The beginning and the end
On Him I can depend
He is my way maker
My strength
No matter what I've faced
He's never lost a case
My rock
My help
The reason I've been kept
My healer
Always faithful
My deliver
Rocks me in the night
The world's brightest light
He is my strength and refuge
My answers are just a few

What if I had asked about your mother?

It would still be the same
Whatever I need Him to be, He becomes that name

Why God Why

Sometimes you may feel life treats you so unfair
So much tragedy it's too much to bear
You look to heaven wondering where is the God that cares
Why God why with your eyes filled with tears
Why would a loving God allow so much suffering and pain
Never any sunshine just heavy rain
No understanding just feeling misunderstood
Why so much bad happens to the good
So many questions but no reply
You continue to ask, why God why

If God revealed why He allows things to happen as they do
It would be too much for our finite brains to grasp a hold to
The fact is we may never fully understand or know why
Our Lord Jesus Christ is merciful, righteous, just, and that we
can't deny
He is never caught in a dilemma or caught by surprise
He is in total control of everything that comes into our lives
What He does is right and He makes no mistakes
Jesus loves us so much that He suffered in our place
Jesus knows from experience our suffering, pains, and aches
God didn't say it would be easy or the load would be light
You must operate by faith and not by sight
He promised if the heavy came to Him, he will give them rest
He promised he would never leave you, He's there during your
test
So it can't be that He doesn't love us or doesn't seem to care
You have to trust His perfect will, stay in faith, and prayer

You Had To Go Through It to Get to It

This world is full of trials and tribulations
It seems as if the devil never takes a vacation
Jesus can show us how to quench the fiery darts he may throw
We must first allow him to be in the driver's seat with total control
Your life maybe in a downward spiral, crisis, or in a bad place
Know that God will get you through every turn and snare by His mercy and grace
No matter the burden your bearing or storm cloud that you face
We must lose our self, follow, serve Him, and His promises we must embrace
There are no shortcuts to get to where God wants you to be
So don't give up or throw in the towel when you're at your red sea
Christ never stopped although He knew what was up ahead
He had to go through it to give us power through the blood that He shed
His power, love, grace, mercy, and strength is sufficient
He will show you how to get through it to get to it, He is omnipotent
There is nothing to hard, big, or small for God, He will teach you to stand
You must go through it to get to it, hold on to His unchanging hand
It's by no means a waste all that you've been through
God had to stir you up and stretch your gift in order to use you
You had to go through it to get to His purpose, plan, and reason
It was all for someone else who is going through their season

Question: What do you do when God is untraceable?

_____

_____

_____

_____

_____

_____

_____

Be strong and courageous. Do not be afraid or terrified because of them, for the LORD your God goes with you; he will never leave you nor forsake you. *Deuteronomy 31:6*

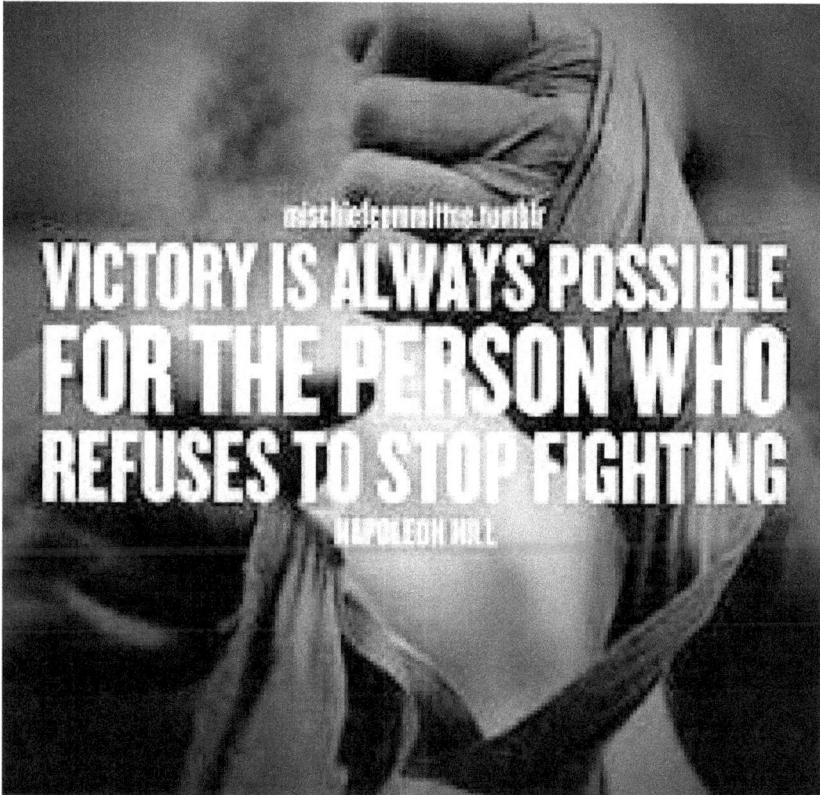

VICTORY IS ALWAYS POSSIBLE FOR THE PERSON WHO REFUSES TO STOP FIGHTING

NAPOLEON HILL

Like Mother Like Daughter Like Father Like Son

We can inherit our mother's eyes
Bone structure, hips, and thighs
We can inherit our father's nose
His big feet and the shape of his toes
We can pick up our parent's characteristics
Become just like them and labeled a statistic
We start to see ourselves in our children when they are young
A bad temper, depression, unforgiveness, or lying tongue
These characteristics go round and round
From our parents, to us, to our children, these spiritual roots are passed down
Some families have the tendency toward infidelity, alcoholism, or divorce
You may think that's just the way I am but your family root is the source
Unlike physical traits these characteristics or tendencies we don't have to receive
In Christ you are a new creature but the devil doesn't want you to believe
The enemy wants you to think like mother like daughter like father like son
My family has always did that and that's the way it's done
These familial habits we must choose to break away
We must denounce the enemy, confess our sin, fast, and pray
We must break the curse off our children's children from generation to generation
From addictions, to homosexuality, down to molestation
Through the power of the Holy Spirit declare to be set free
Not entangled with the yoke of bondage the word you must decree
No longer like mother like daughter, like father like son, or the family's sin
Set free in Jesus and heirs of God, a new life to begin

Stronghold

A stronghold of Satan attaches to someone and refuses to depart
A stronghold isn't there for beneficial purposes but to tear your mind apart
It only surrenders when Christ powers are exerted against it
Strongholds manifest in the form of worry, unnatural thoughts, oppression, or evil desires that are persistent
Their only intent is to harass, burden, unnerve, and to cause affliction
Know this can be broken because of Jesus Christ crucifixion
First step to breaking a stronghold is you must know your authority to do so
Christ granted you the power to defeat the enemy of your life over two thousand years ago
It's your authority to declare that spiritual power of darkness will not lord over you
As a believer in Jesus Christ you must confess Jesus is Lord and that's what you must attest to
Secondly, exercise your faith over the stronghold
Recognize who you are, believe God, and be bold
The devil is defeated on the battlefield
When your faith in Christ is your shield
Lastly, demonstrate God's mighty power
He parted the red sea and dried up rivers, the same God of yesterday is this very hour
Know your authority over satan, he only comes to deceive
God will give you the victory over him, His word you must believe
Don't be afraid to confront your stronghold
Recognize your authority and be bold

The Thief

There is a thief who's on the loose
Our spiritual blessings he wants to rob
He makes it his priority and number one job
Jesus warned us of what the devil wants to fulfill
In John 10:10 he comes to rob, destroy, and kill

One of our spiritual blessings he wants to rob is our peace
Here are just a few ways he tries to get our peace to cease
He sends temptation to allure us to sin
He knows we'll lose our peace with God if we give in

The thief can't stand for us to be in perfect peace
Not even in our bodies he'll send a sickness or disease
He can't stand peace in our soul so he taunts and torments our mind
Sending negative words and thoughts of all kind
He knows God commands a blessing when brethren dwell in unity
So he will sow lies, envy, strife, and selfishness when given the opportunity
He sets up misunderstandings and offenses to come against the vision
He wants to steal the peace that God desires among the church to cause division
2 Corinthians 2:11 we must not be ignorant of the devil devises or scheme
We as Gods victorious army must rise and say enough, we are the redeemed
Our peace doesn't belong to the enemy, his camp we must attack
Declaring Jesus purchased it on the cross and we want it back

We have the power, strength, and anointing through Christ to be bold
Give me back my peace and everything else that you stole

Don't let the devil come into your church life, family, or homes
To and fro back after your peace, beware of the thief that roams

Words

Bless or curse
Speak life or death
Build up or tear down
Make whole or dismember
Positive or negative words are forever remembered
They pierce like a sword
Cut sharp like a knife
Straight through the heart words do slice
Truth or lie
Gentle or harsh
Good or evil
The words that go forth are irretrievable
They ignite intensively a raging fire
Polluting the body from the smoke
Choking out its victim by the words that was spoke

"Depart from me" the earth opened her mouth and they went down into the pit

Terrifying darkness
Punishment
Fearsome noises
Loud cries
Screams
Weeping and gnashing of teeth
They refused God on earth now their souls down beneath
Wailing
Burning
Everlasting flames
Eternity torment
The stench of souls burning scent
The fire is never quenched
Their worm never dies
Repent or in hell you will lift up thine eyes

Damnation of Hell

Question: In what ways can you overcome the giants in your life?

_____

_____

_____

_____

_____

_____

_____

_____

Above all, taking the shield of faith, wherewith ye shall be able to quench all the fiery darts of the wicked. *Ephesians 6:16*

My Testimony

Only GOD can turn a MESS into a MESSAGE..
A TEST into a TESTIMONY..
A TRIAL into a TRIUMPH..
a VICTIM into a VICTORY!!

Tears from a Touch

A woman now, it's a faded scar
Lord you didn't leave me after bringing me this far
As I look back over the years
I see times when my life was full with tears
When I was born I was told I cried
Was that the day misery crept inside
K through fifth I can't complain
It was sixth through tenth I felt insane
As a young girl the tears began to roll
Down my face uncontrollable they flowed
The first thunderously fell from my chin then more
They created a puddle on the floor
In the reflection a word I could see
Wholeness rippled away at me
Twelve years of age
Another tearful page
Age thirteen rage screamed though my tears
They were so loud but no one seemed to hear
One, two, three times suicide went wrong
So many around yet I was all alone
I wanted to just fly away and make heaven my home
Fourteen, I couldn't take anymore
Bloodshed tears as I kneeled before the lord
Fifteen years old an angel appeared
Came for my pillow full of tears
Squeezed them into an alabaster box
A voice whispered, priceless is the cost
Not one of your tears was ever lost
You no longer have to fear anymore
From this day forth I've closed the door
Hyssop I've put on your wound
Healing to follow real soon
I will never forsake you, I am here
Just call upon me, I am near
I had to allow that trial for you
So that you would be able to pull others through

Weeping did endure for a night
Joy came in the morning light
Heaviness I did replace
Upon you now the garment of praise
Daughter of Zion this day I've raised

Question: What is your testimony and how has it helped others?

_____

_____

_____

_____

_____

_____

_____

_____

And they overcame him by the blood of the Lamb, and by the word of
their testimony; and they loved not their lives unto the death.
Revelations 12:11

About the author

Michelle E. Medley is a freelance writer and poet. She loves to encourage and to be inspired. She knows from her own life experiences that whatever it is you may be going through, whatever the challenge you may be facing, whatever it is that's stopping you from reaching your dreams and goals, it's just a matter of time that you will overcome these temporary obstacles as she has. She lives in Tennessee with her husband, four children, and grandson. Her latest project is Manifested from the Soul she is compiling that will be published next year. Contact Michelle at michelleemedley@yahoo.com

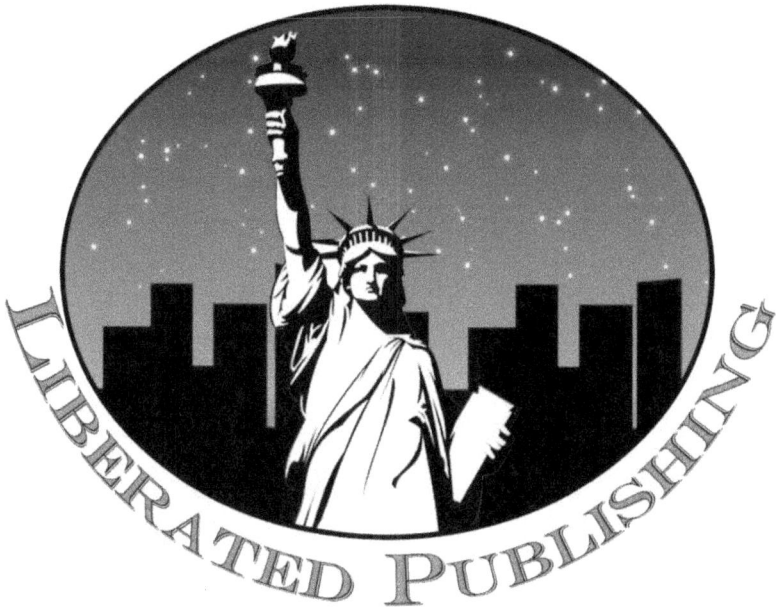

Liberated Publishing Inc
1860 Wilma Rudolph Blvd
Clarksville, TN 37040
info@liberatedpublishing.com
931-378-0500

www.LiberatedPublishing.com

www.ingramcontent.com/pod-product-compliance
Lightning Source LLC
LaVergne TN
LVHW021358080426
835508LV00020B/2341